PROGRESSIVE
BASS
LICKS

BY STEPHAN RICHTER

60 MINUTE STEREO
CASSETTE AVAILABLE

All the examples in Progressive Bass Licks
have been recorded on to a 60 minute STEREO
cassette tape.

ZENITH
MUSIC
Stirling Highway
Claremont 6010
Western Australia

Acknowledgements

Cover: Phil Martin
Rock Photographs: Neil Zlozower
Instruments supplied by Derringers Music

Distributed by

in **Australia**
Koala Publications Pty. Ltd.
4 Captain Cook Ave.
Flinders Park 5025
South Australia
Ph (08) 268 1750
Fax 61-8-352-4760

in **U.S.A.**
Koala Publications Inc.
3001 Redhill Ave.
Bldg. 2 # 104
Costa Mesa CA
U.S.A. 92626
Ph (714) 546 2743
Fax 1-714-546-2749

in **U.K. and Europe**
Music Exchange
Claverton Rd.
Wythenshawe
Manchester
M23 9NE
England
Ph (061) 946 1234
Fax (061) 946 1195

ISBN 0 947183 72 8

Contents

Introduction 4

Symbols, Abbreviations and Tablature 5,6

Rock – Straight and Syncopation 7

Blues – Major, Hammer-on and Minor Licks 8

Heavy Metal 9

Shuffle 10

Reggae – Triplet and Straight Feel 12

Reggae Shuffle and Ghost Notes 13

Triplet Rock 14

Jazz – Walking Bass, Half Time Feel, Syncopation 15

Funk 16

Rap 19

Latin – Different Syncopated Licks Including Salsa 21

Harmonics – Fretboard Chart, Major Triads and
                Combination with Fretted Playing Notes 25

$\frac{6}{8}$ Time and Afro Rhythms 29

Odd Time $\frac{5}{4}$, $\frac{7}{4}$ 32

Time Displacement 33

Alternating Between Two Grooves 34

Left Hand Stretch 36

Runs and Arpeggios – Blues-Rock, Ascending, Descending,
    Major, Minor, Two Octave Playing and Transposition 37

Vibrato-Shake 42

More Licks, Grooves, Runs and Bass Lines –
    in various styles, including $\frac{12}{8}$ time 43

Chord Progressions, Different Bass Lines and Licks –
    featuring all styles played so far and some new ones 50

Detuning to the Low D 60

Slap in Different Styles 61

Tapping 64

Introduction

Progressive Bass Licks features over 190 licks which use most modern music styles and techniques used by the world's best bass players. Before using this book and cassette it is important to have some practical experience playing the bass guitar (see *Progressive Bass Guitar* by Gary Turner and Brenton White or *Heavy Metal Method for Bass* by Stephan Richter).

The emphasis in this volume is to provide a vast variety of music styles to enable you to fit in with any music performing or recording situation. It is not necessary to work through every page before proceeding to the next, as it depends on what area you want to improve your skills. However, some of the styles and techniques may require more time and explanation according to your personal standard and therefore, it is suggested you use some of the other bass guitar books of the Progressive series mentioned below.

The Licks in these books are particularly useful as reinforcements of:

1) Technical aspects of playing bass.
2) A source of ideas for your own licks and solos.
3) Practical exercises.
4) A source of teaching material.

It is important that after a while you begin to play these licks with some variations of your own. Combine the study of these licks with constant playing and listening. All bass players use the same basics, but development of style is determined by how these basics are used.

Both music and TAB notation are used. For music readers most of the licks have accidentals (sharps, flats) placed in front of the note to be played. In some cases a key signature is used. For more information on key signatures, reading music and TAB notation see *Progressive Bass Guitar*.

Chord symbols are used to give an indication of what a guitarist or keyboarder would play and how the bass line relates to chords.

The technique to use is mentioned above each lick e.g. use of hammer-on, etc. If nothing is specified use your right hand fingers to play the lick. To make reading easier and to find the notes faster on the fretboard, tablature notation is used. Also fingering numbers are used to help you find the easiest way of playing a lick.

Due to the speed, phrasing and range of some bass licks they are quite often very hard to read from written music. For this reason it is essential to have the cassette tape that contains all the examples in this book. The book tells you where to locate your fingers and what technique to use, and the tape lets you hear how the lick should sound.

Good luck and have fun.

Stephan Richter

Stephan Richter obtained his degree in Classical Music (Cello major) at the Zurich Conservatorium of Music in Switzerland. He further studied in New York on Electric Bass with Rick Laird and Tony Oppenheim. He currently works as a session musician and teacher. Stephan is author of Progressive Slap Technique for Bass, Tapping Technique for Bass, Heavy Metal Method and Heavy Metal Techniques for Bass, and Heavy Metal Licks Volume 1 and 2.

Symbols and Abbreviations

The Left Hand

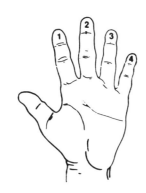

1 = Index finger

2 = Middle finger

3 = Ring finger

4 = Little finger

The Right Hand

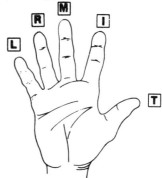

T = Thumb finger

I = Index finger

M = Middle finger

R = Ring finger

L = Little finger

  staccato (short detached note)

 Hammer-on; generate the sound of a note with the force of your "fretting" finger. Do not "pick" the note.

  Quick Hammer-on

  Shift between notes

  Slide - into the indicated note

  Slide - only the first note is picked

  Slide - commence the slide somewhere further up the neck

  Slide - quick

Symbols and Abbreviations (cont.)

PO   Pull-off

〜〜〜   Vibrato

×   Ghost Notes - mute

>   Accent – play louder

Up-strum or raking

Down-strum or raking

Harmonic

T   Thumb slap or tap with the thumb

P   Popping Effect

Left Hand Stretch

HA   Hammer Attack

↓   Tapping right hand

[I]   Tapping using Index finger

[I]
[M]   Tapping Index and Middle finger together

Tablature

Tablature is a method of indicating the position of notes on the fretboard. There are four "tab" lines, each representing one of the four strings on the bass.

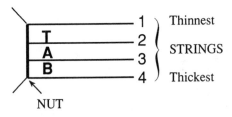

When a number is placed on one of the lines, it indicates the fret location of a note, e.g.

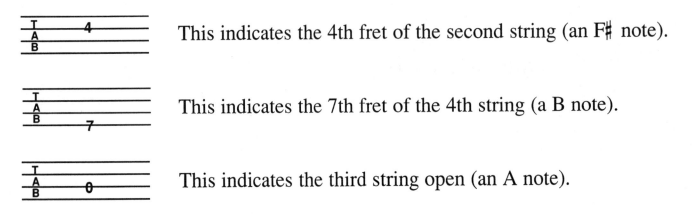

This indicates the 4th fret of the second string (an F♯ note).

This indicates the 7th fret of the 4th string (a B note).

This indicates the third string open (an A note).

Rock
Accent on one and three, simple chords.

Lick 1 and 2 use a straight eighth note feel.

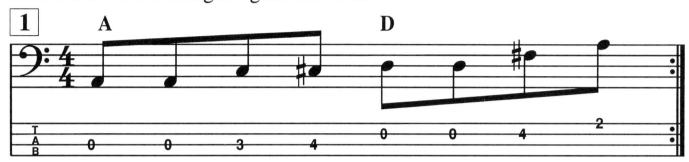

Lick 3 uses more repeated eighth notes.

Lick 4 uses quarter notes, eighth notes and syncopation.

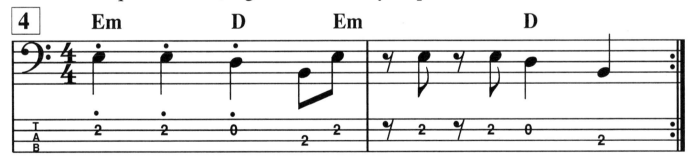

Lick 5 uses more syncopation.

Blues

**Uses notes of the blues or pentatonic scale,
normally based upon a form of 12 bars.**

Lick 6 uses notes of the Major pentatonic scale.

Lick 7 uses Hammer-ons and minor and Major 3rds after each other, which creates the "bluesy" sound.

Lick 8 is a minor pentatonic blues run.

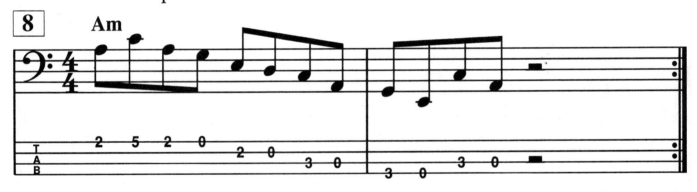

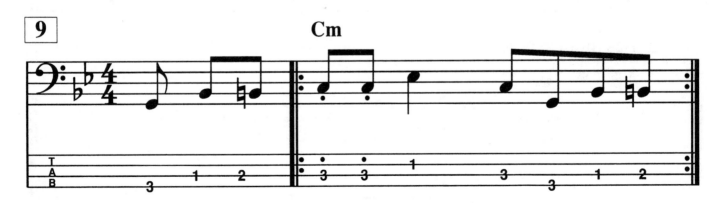

Heavy Metal
Different influences from Hard Rock to Classical etc.

Lick 10 uses a rhythm and descending melodic movement which is very common in Heavy Metal.

Lick 12 uses a triplet feel.

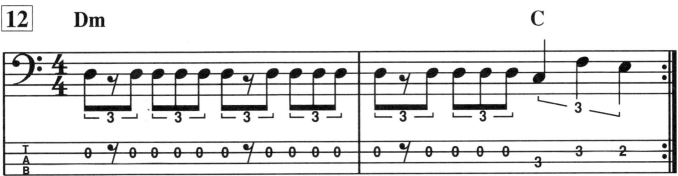

Lick 13 is a Heavy Metal bass run.

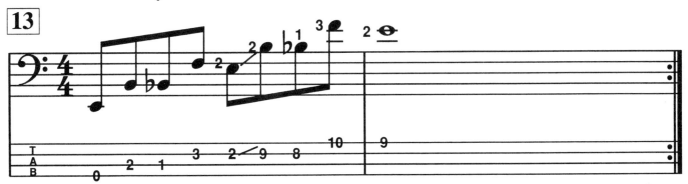

For more information on Heavy Metal see Progressive Heavy Metal Method, Technique and Licks Vol. I and II by Stephan Richter.

Shuffle
Accent on one and three with a triplet feel – can occur in Rock, Blues etc.

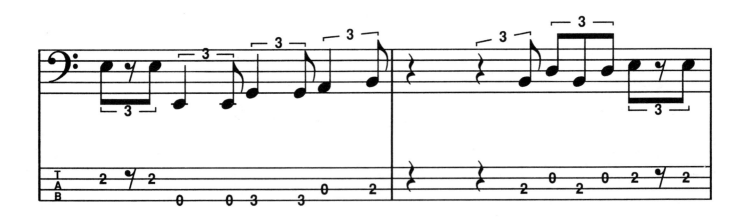

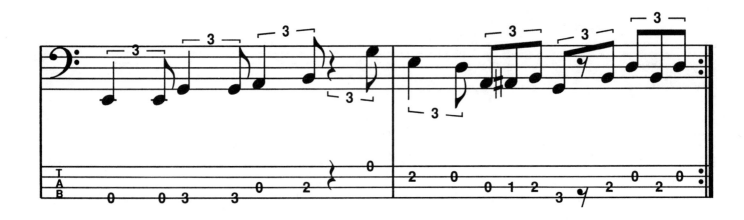

15 **E7#9**

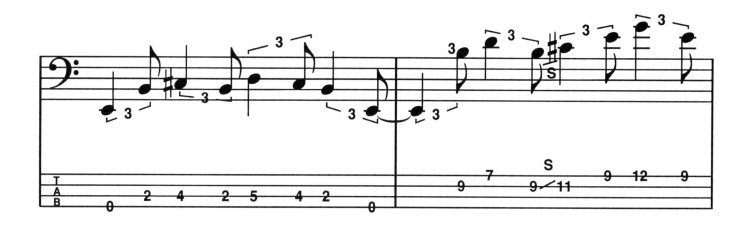

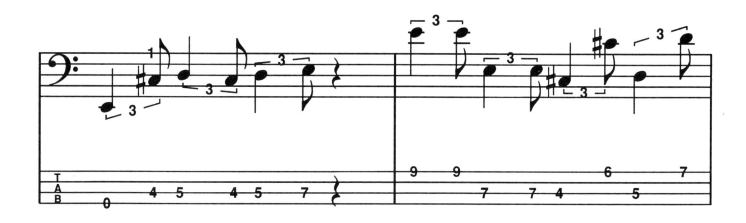

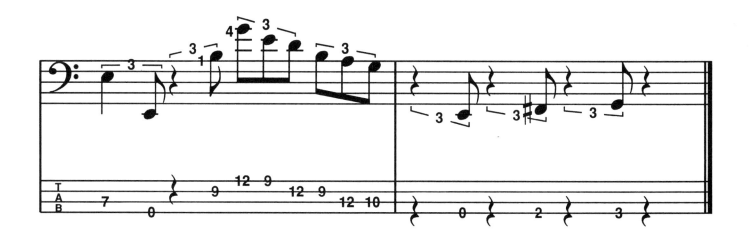

Reggae
Jamaican rhythm with rhythmic emphasis placed on the off beats.

Straight Reggae feel.

Reggae Shuffle

*Ghost notes. For more information on ghost notes see Heavy Metal Technique or Slap Technique.

Triplet Rock

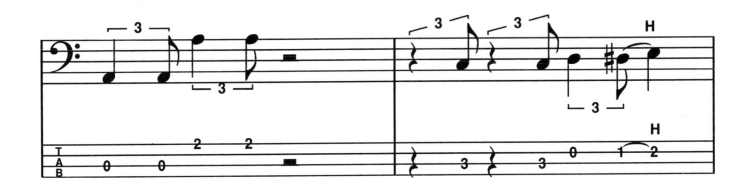

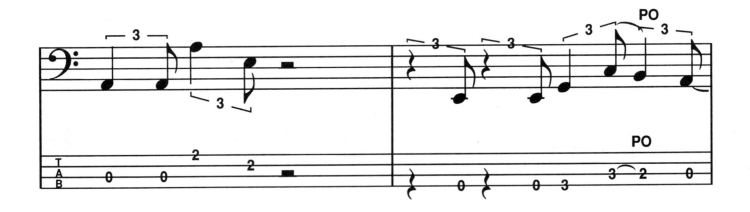

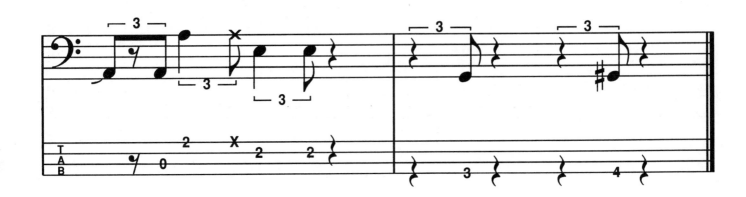

Jazz

Triplet feel incorporating more advanced rhythms and harmony. Many jazz tunes use a swing feel which have a walking bass line.

Walking bass – bass line predominantly playing every beat (quarter note) in $\frac{4}{4}$ time in a linear fashion.

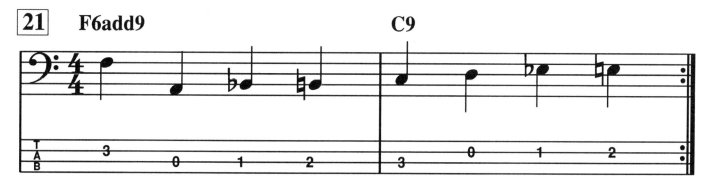

The next three examples use a very common jazz chord progression.

Half time feel – dividing the bar in two rather than four (half notes, dotted notes etc.)

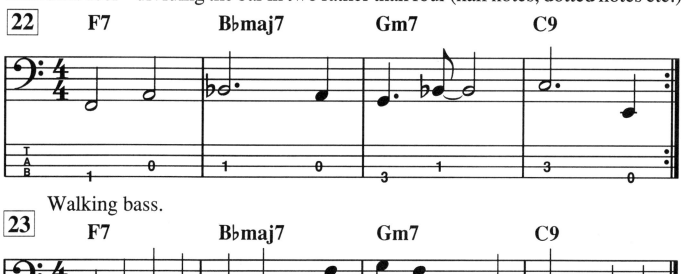

Example 24 is a walking bass with triplets, ghost notes and syncopation.

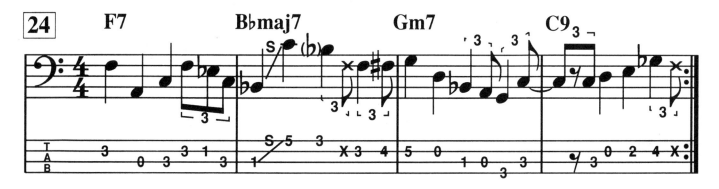

Funk

Accent on one and three, staccato feel using sixteenth notes, syncopation and anticipation.

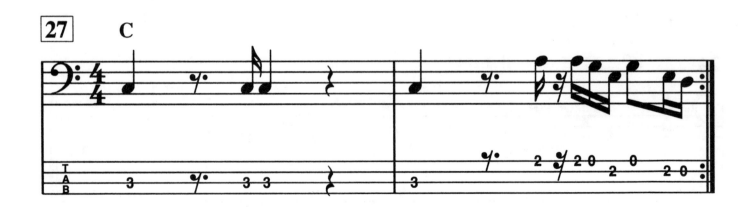

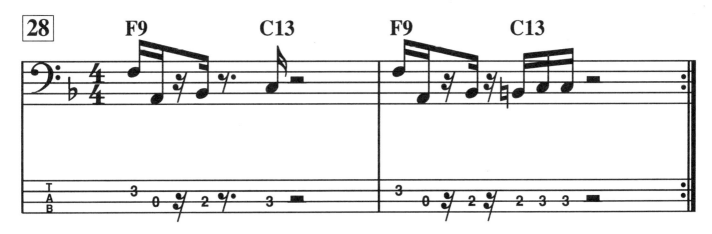

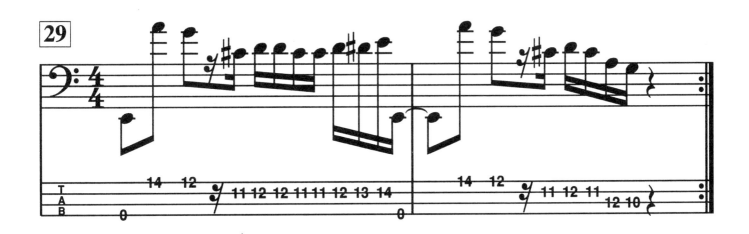

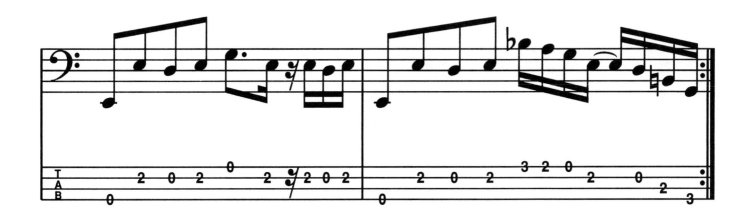

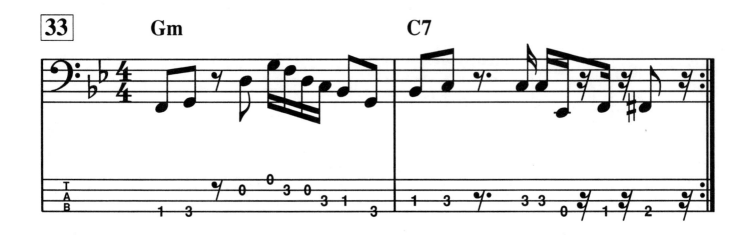

Rap

Incorporating characteristics of Rock and Funk styles.

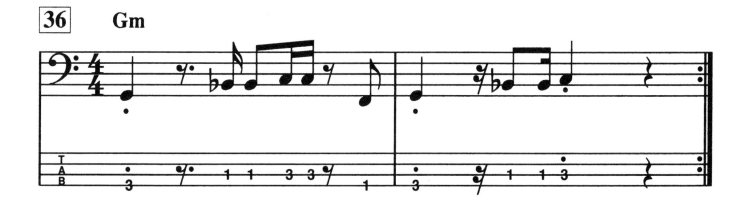

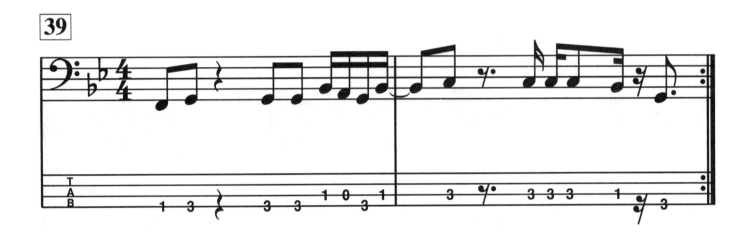

Geddy Lee (Rush)

Mark Egan

Latin

Rhythms founded in Latin America which use a straight feel with emphasis on off beats.

40   Am7

G7

Salsa – Afro Cuban rhythm accent on "2" and "4+".

41   Dm   Dm/C♯   Dm/C   Dm/B

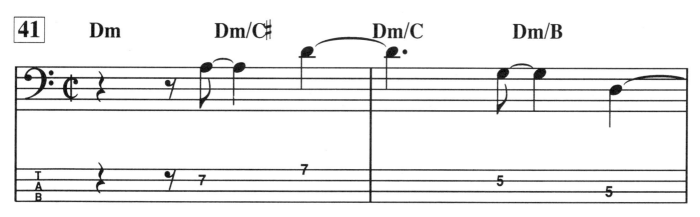

Dm   Dm/C♯   Dm/C   Dm/B

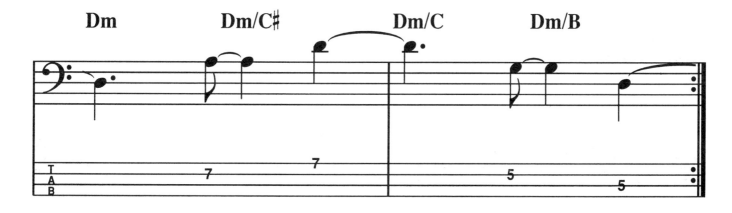

22

The bass line below is normally doubled with the piano or keyboard.

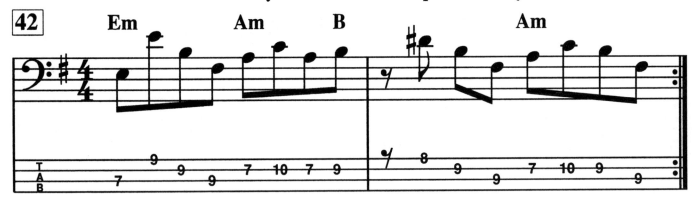

The next bass line is based upon the same chord progression as the last one.
Both lines can be played together, as one is more like a piano and the other is like
a bass line.

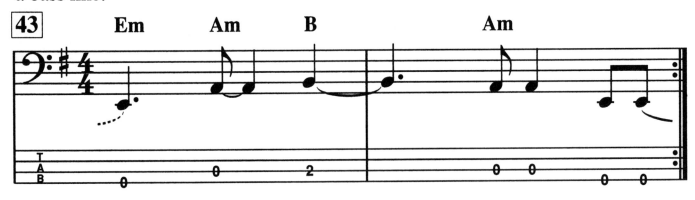

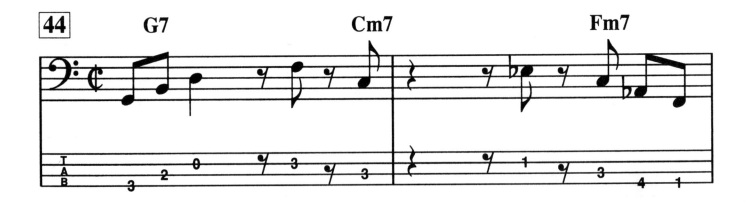

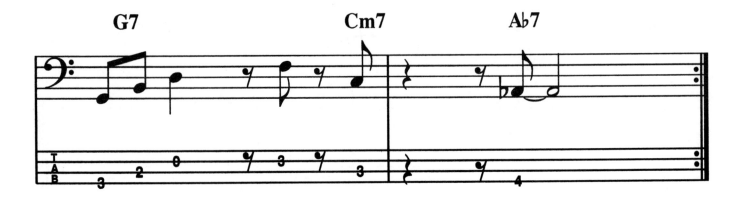

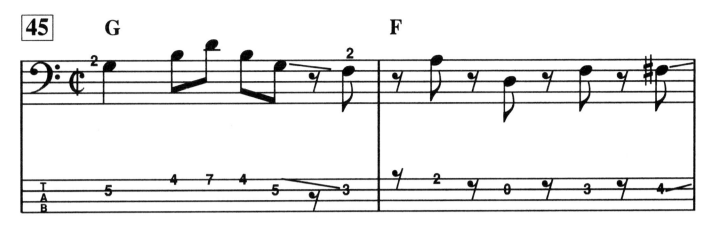

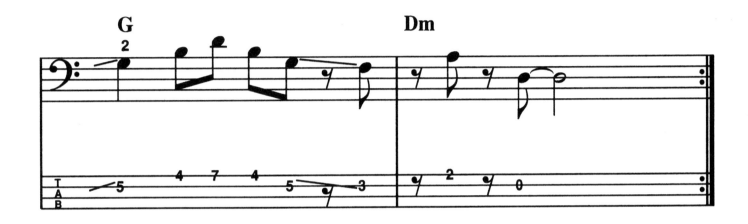

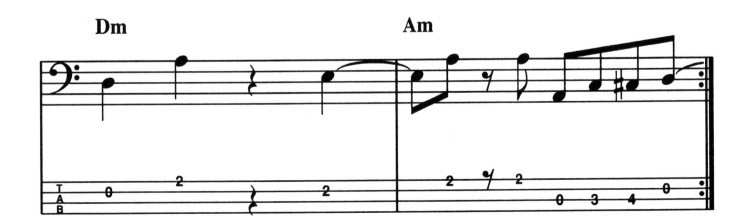

Harmonics

In this section harmonics are used (indicated ♪).

A harmonic is a chime like sound created by lightly touching a vibrating string with the left hand at certain points along the fretboard. For the best results pluck the string near the bridge and boost the treble control. The most common harmonics are found on the 12th, 7th and 5th frets.

Below is a chart which shows you where to obtain harmonics on the fret board.

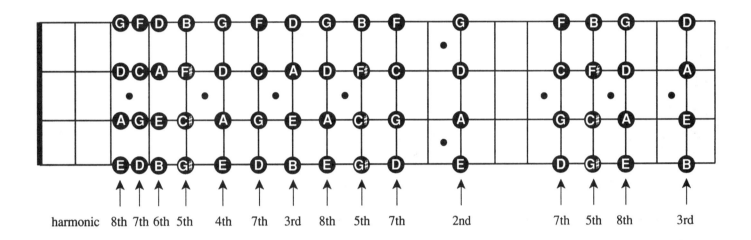

John Patitucci

Major Triads on one string.

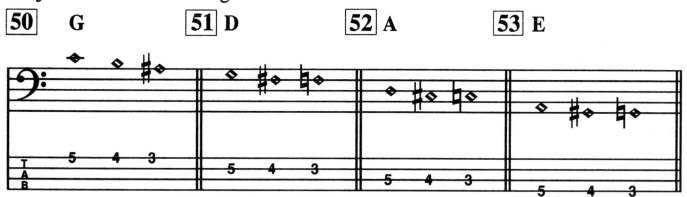

The next five licks use all the harmonics on the 7th fret across all 4 strings.
Make up your own combinations.

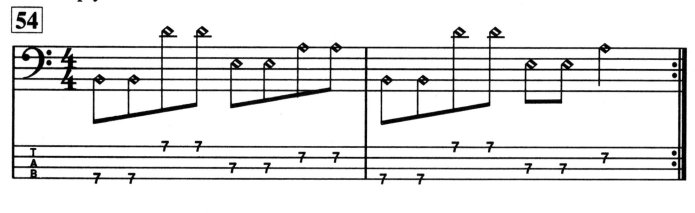

Use the raking technique for the next three examples.

For more information on raking technique see Heavy Metal Technique.

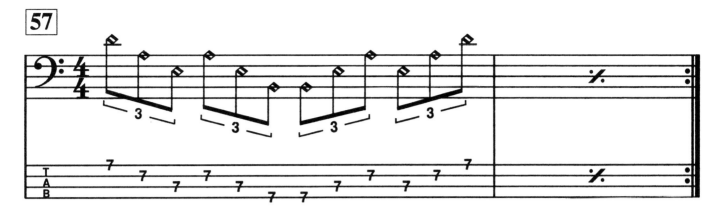

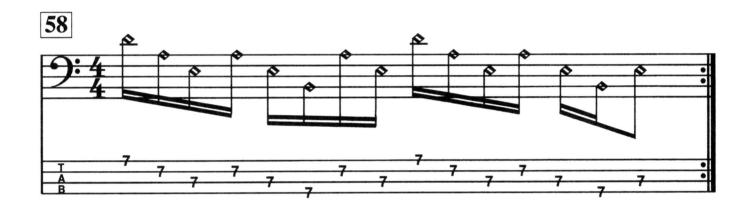

Lick 59 uses a combination of harmonics and fretted notes.

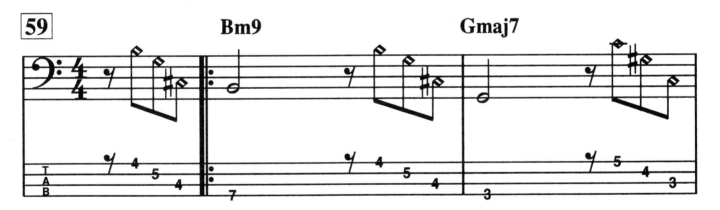

Let all notes ring!

Lick 60 again uses a combination of harmonics and fretted notes.

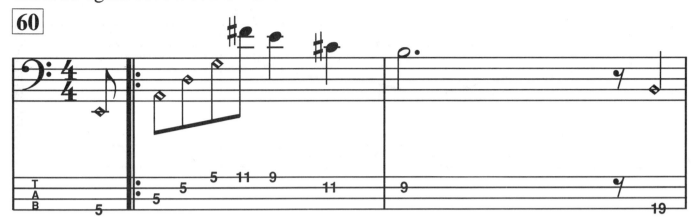

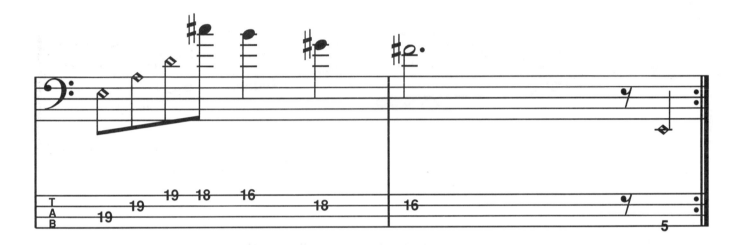

Joe Satriani & Stu Hamm

$\frac{6}{8}$ Time and Afro Rhythms

Afro rhythms predominantly in $\frac{6}{8}$ with rhythmical emphasis on the off beats.

The next eight examples use the same chord progression.

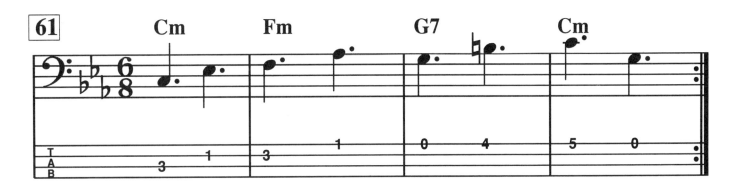

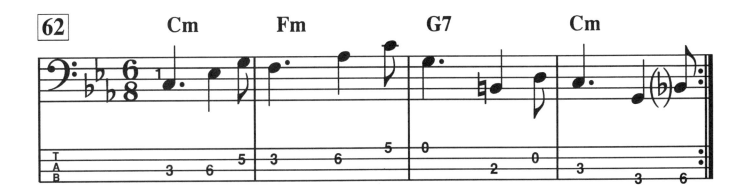

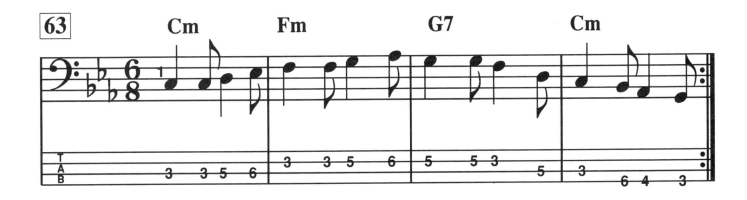

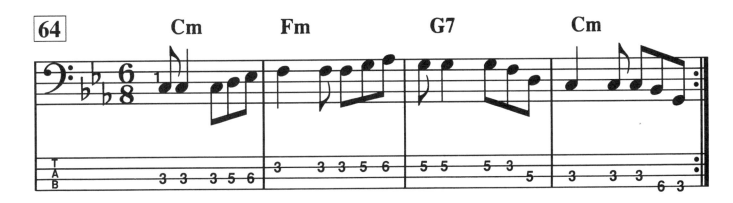

Afro

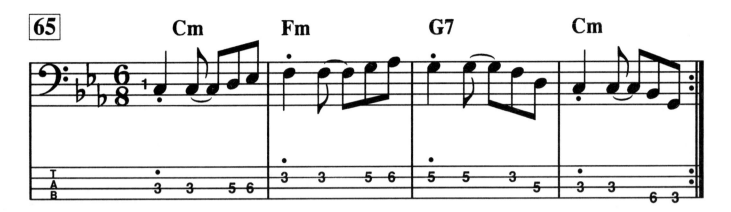

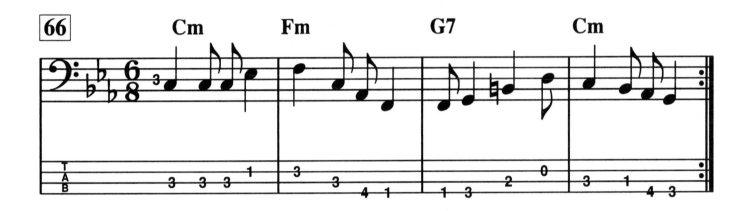

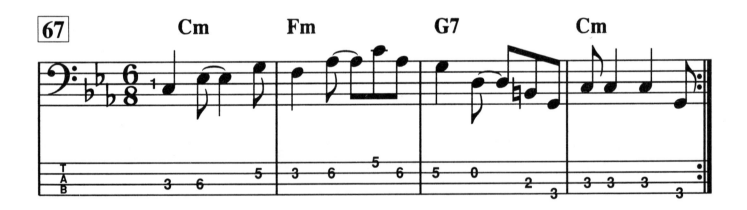

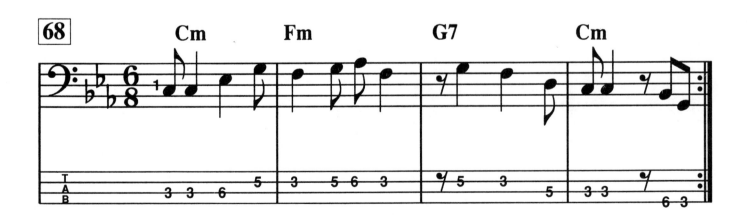

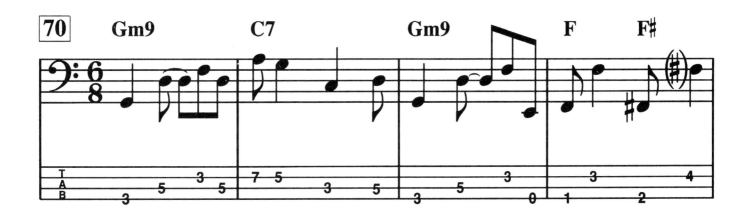

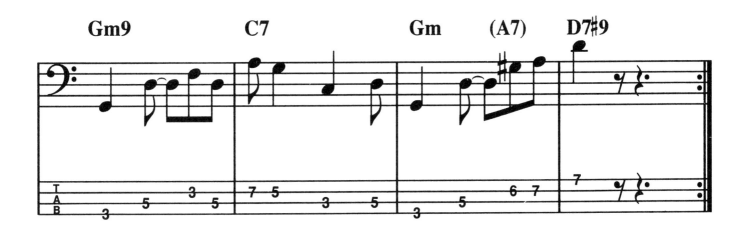

Lick 71 is in $\frac{4}{4}$ time using sixteeth notes with an African flavoured sound.

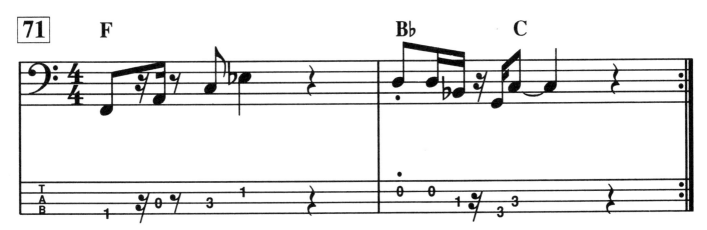

Odd Time

**Any rhythm whose time signature contains an odd number
in the nominator (top digit) e.g. $\frac{5}{4}$, $\frac{7}{4}$.**

72

73

Steve Harris (Iron Maiden)

Time Displacement

Time displacement occurs when a rhythmic or melodic phrase is repeated and has its starting point occurring on a different beat.

Lick 74 uses the time displacement concept indicated with the ⦙ in the middle.

74

75

76

Lick 77 uses a combination of different timings.

77

Alternating Between Two Grooves

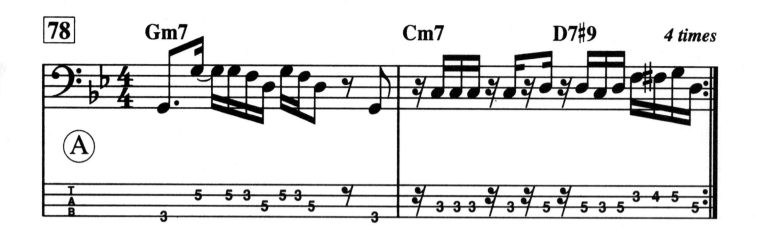

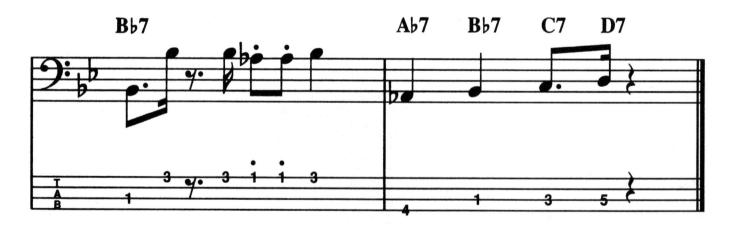

back to Ⓐ

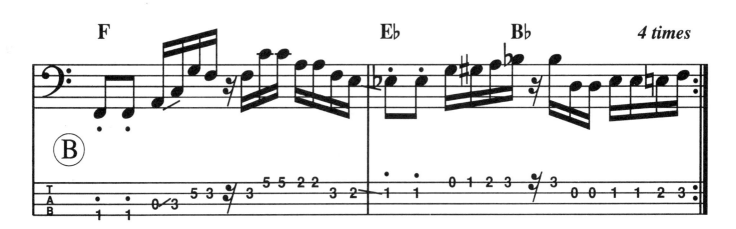

back to Ⓐ

Jach Bruce (Cream)   Billy Sheehan (Mr. Big)

Left Hand Stretch (indicated by ✕)

Stretch between your first and second finger as indicated in the examples below.
Normal space is 1 fret (or semitone), a stretch is 2 frets (or tone).

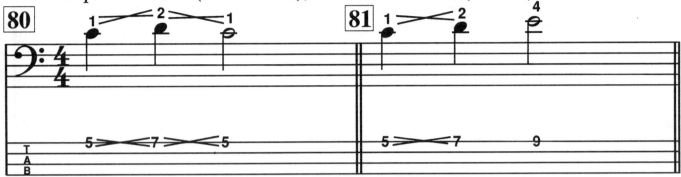

In Lick 82 the first bar uses the stretch.

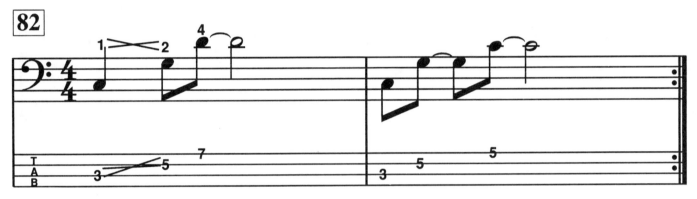

The next example is a variation of Lick 82 using ghost notes.

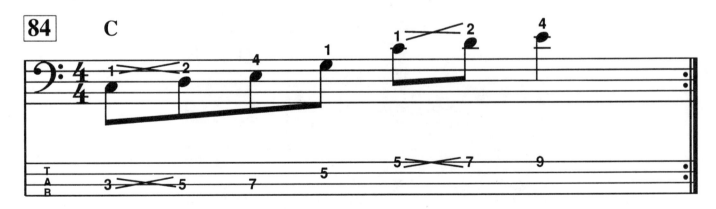

The left hand stretch technique will expand your playing ability.
Experiment with it!

Runs and Arpeggios

Blues/Rock.

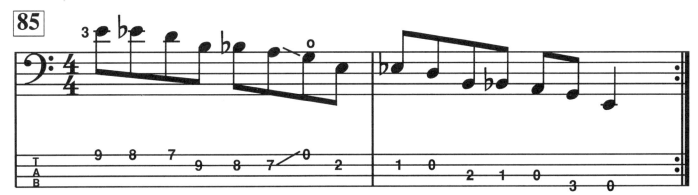

Fast.

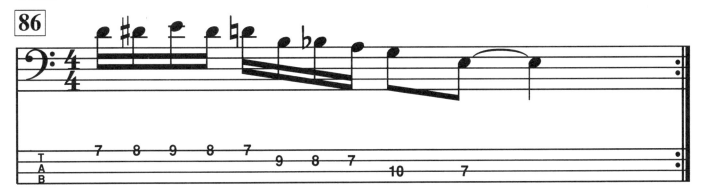

Descending E Major run.

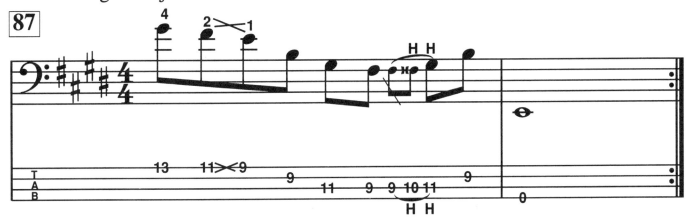

Ascending D minor.

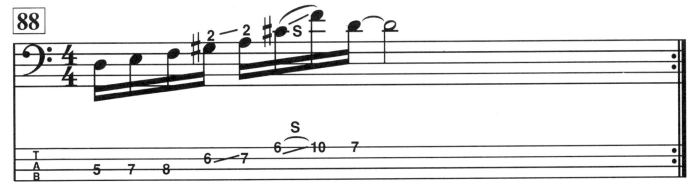

Lick 89 is in a Major key.

Lick 90 is in a minor key.

Melodic Arpeggio run.

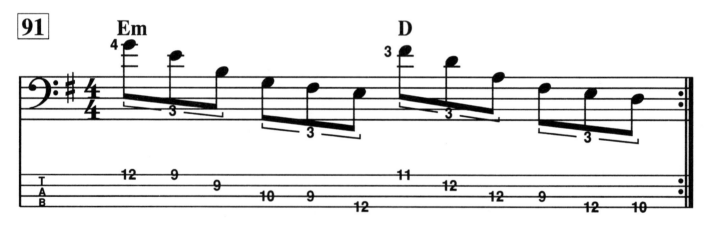

Lick 92 is a variation of the previous lick.

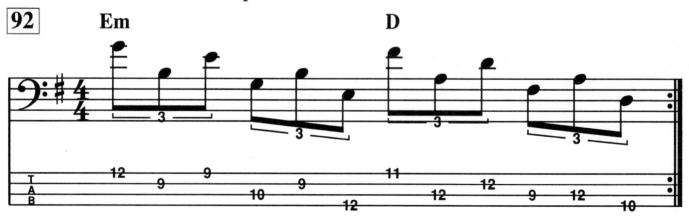

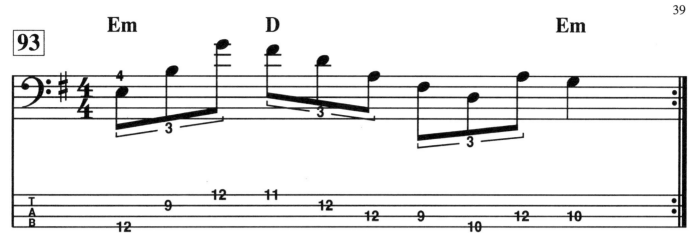

Arpeggio run over two octaves.

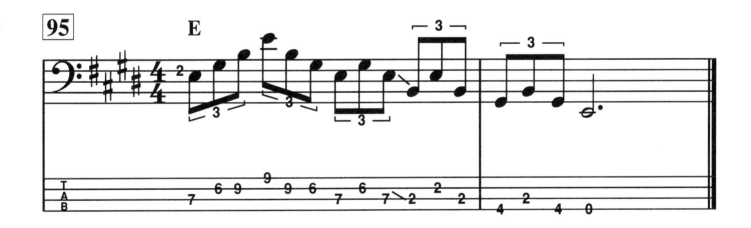

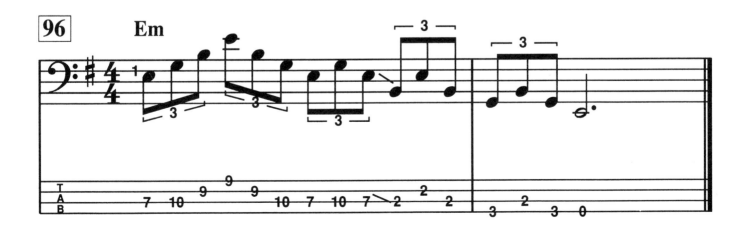

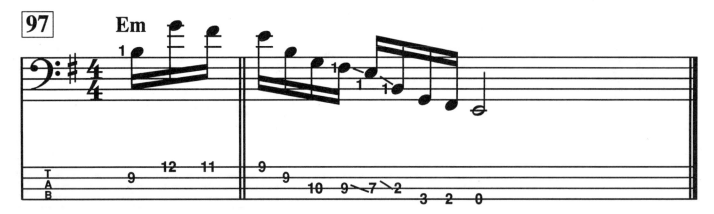

The next three runs are transpositions of each other.

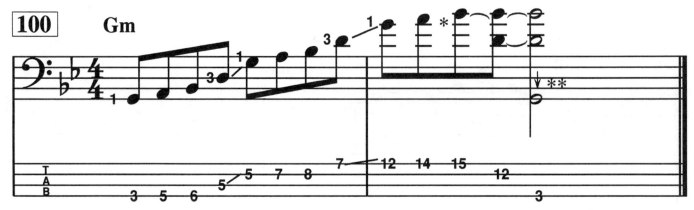

* Let the last three notes ring as a chord in Exercises 98, 99 and 100.

**↓ Right hand cross tapping (see Heavy Metal Technique).

The next three examples use time displacement.
See also Lick 14 (Shuffle beat), Funk Lick 30 and Lick 74 for time displacement.

In Lick 101 the second bar uses the same notes but on the off beat.

In Lick 102 the notes of the second bar are one sixteenth note ahead.

Compare all bars to each other to see the time shift.

Vibrato Shake 〰

* The vibrato shake is the technique of shifting rapidly backwards and forwards from the playing note to the next highest fret.

Listen to the tape.

104

105

Metallica

More Licks, Grooves, Runs and Bass Lines in Various Styles

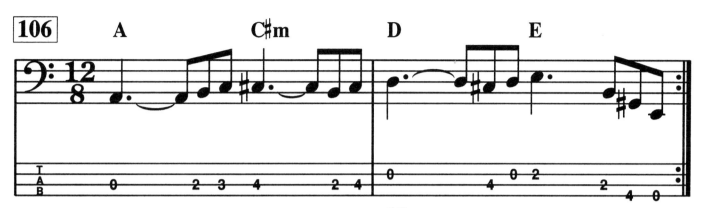

The above lick is a slow Blues, Rock feel in $\frac{12}{8}$ time.

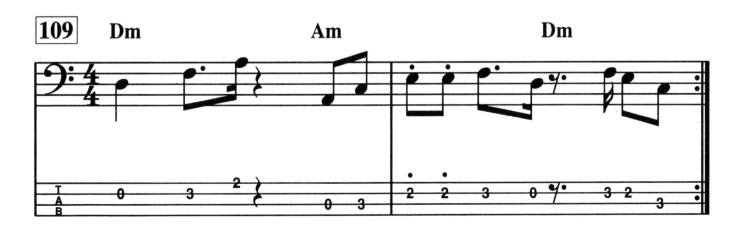

44

The next two examples are based upon the same chord progression.

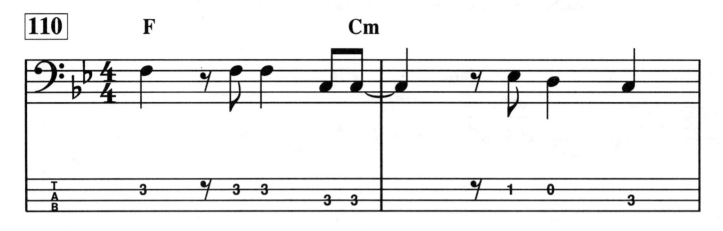

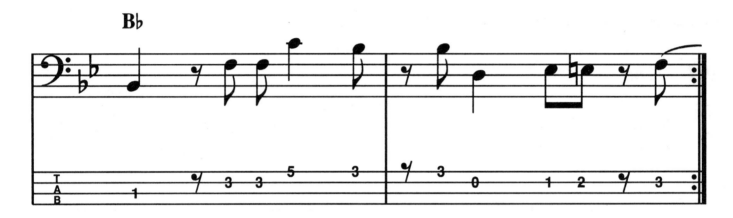

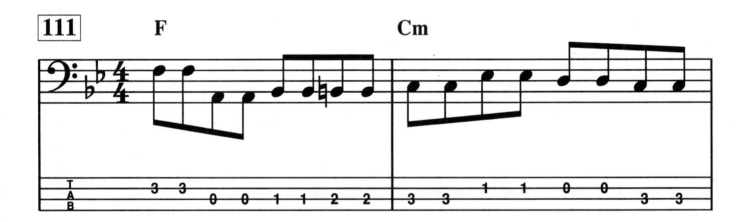

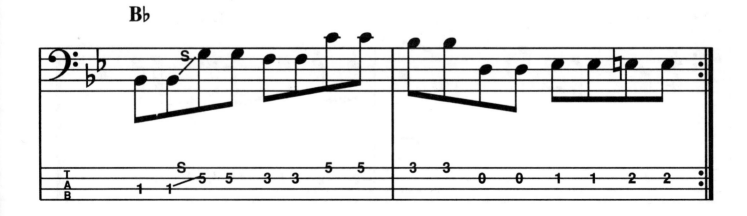

112

The next two examples are based upon the same chord progression.

113

114

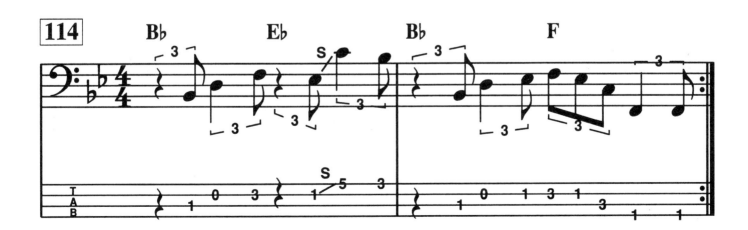

115

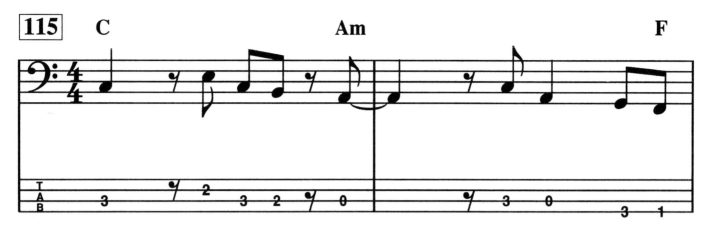

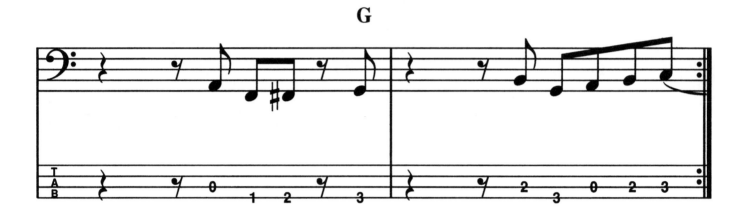

Lick 116 and 117 are in E.

116

117

118   F

Lick 119 is in A minor.

119

120

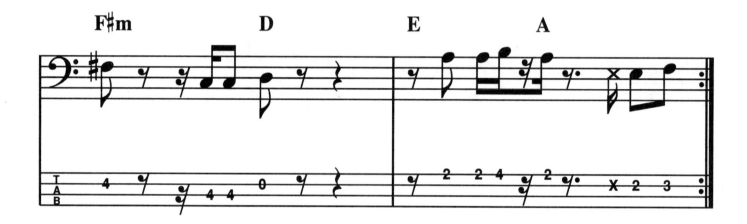

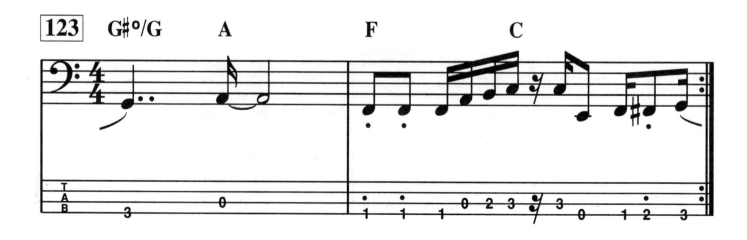

124

125

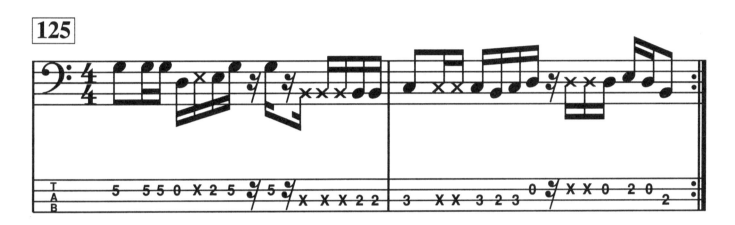

Paul McCartney

Chord Progressions, Different Bass Lines and Licks
featuring all styles played so far and some new ones.

The next six examples use the same chord progression.

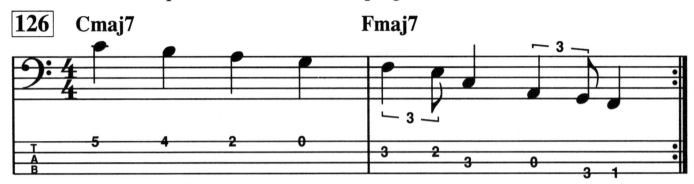

Rock.

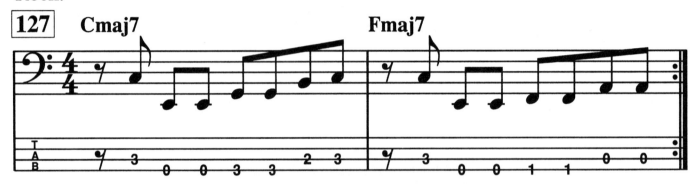

Arpeggio run with a Latin feel.

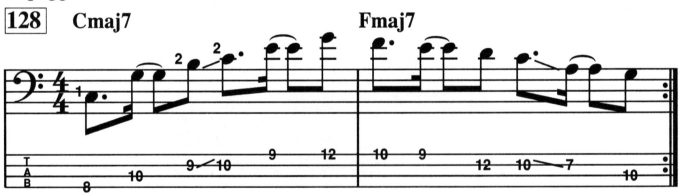

Harmonics chord.

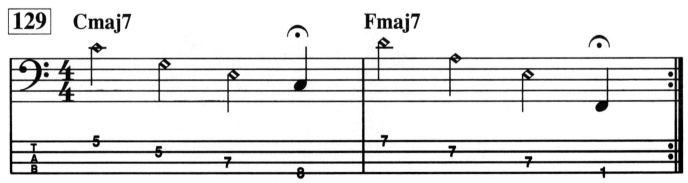

Let all notes ring!

Arpeggio run.

Funk.

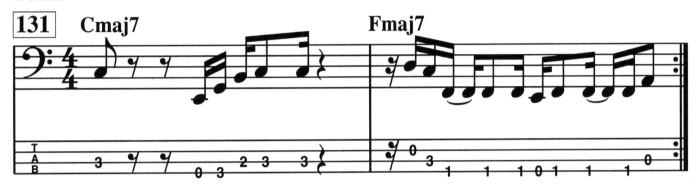

The next seven examples are based upon the same chord progression.

Rock.

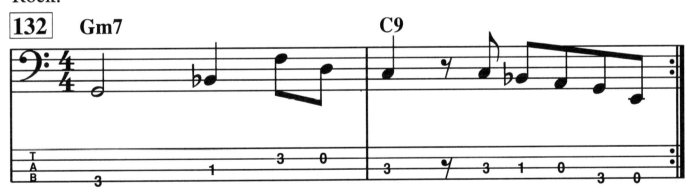

Jazz.

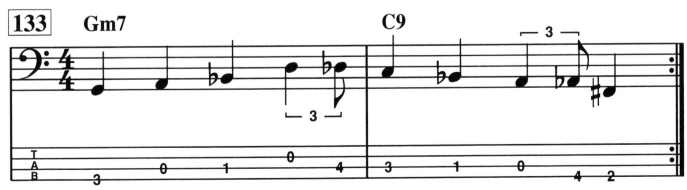

Jazz.

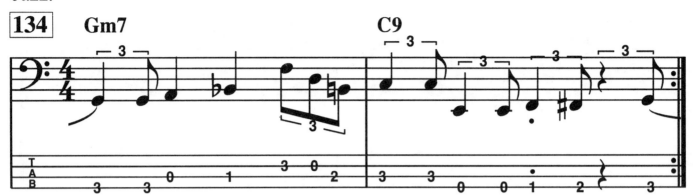

Latin Rock.

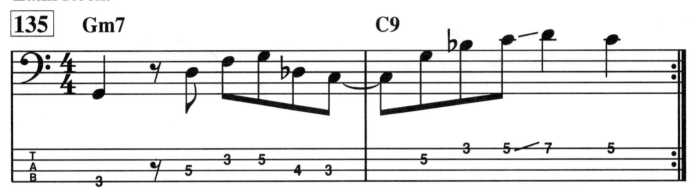

Funky Rock.

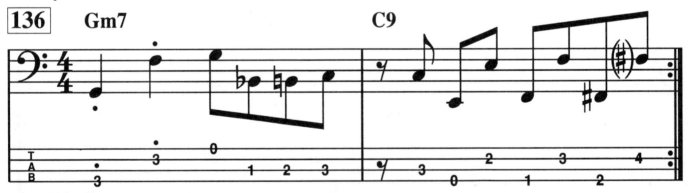

Off beat playing.

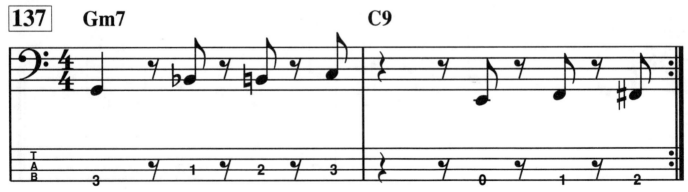

Funk.

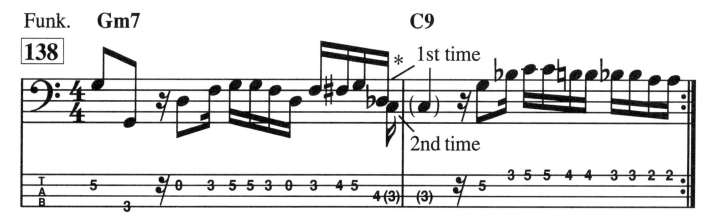

*The first time through play the Db as indicated, and the second time through replace it with the C note, (then omit the C note in brackets on the down beat).

The next seven examples are based upon the same chord progression.
Bossa Nova – syncopated Brazilian rhythm, usually medium tempo.

Samba –style of Brazilian music which has a rhythmic emphasis on one and three, played by one or more members of the band. The tempo ranges from medium to very fast.

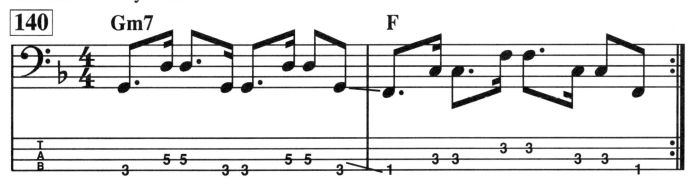

Rock.

54

Latin Rock.

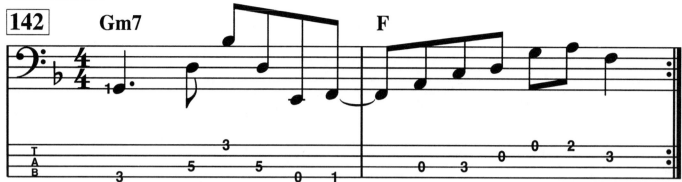

Fusion – combination of Rock, Jazz, Latin etc.

Jazz.

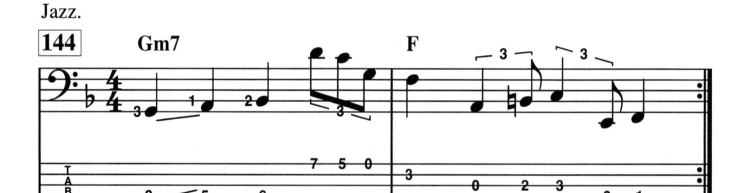

Afro.

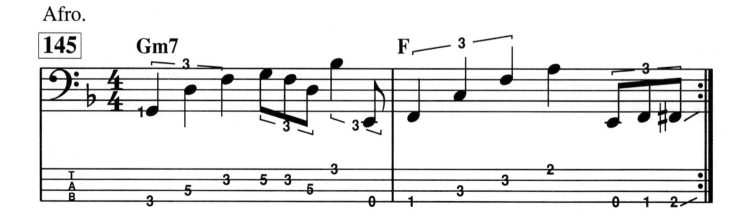

The next three examples use a slight variation of the chord progression.

Rock.

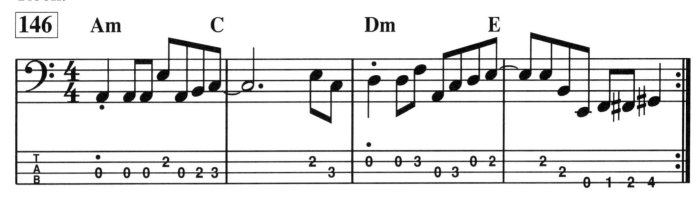

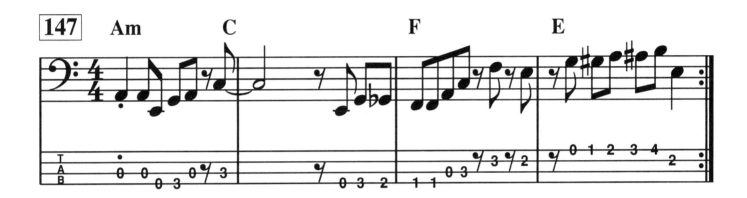

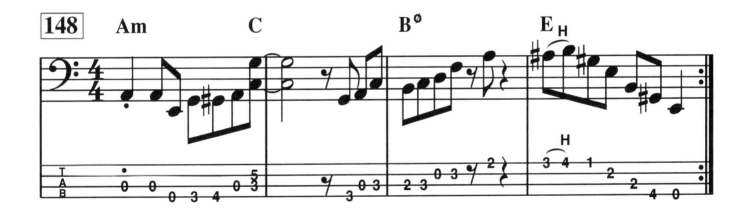

Hard Rock.

The next six examples are based upon the same chord progression.

Rock Jazz.

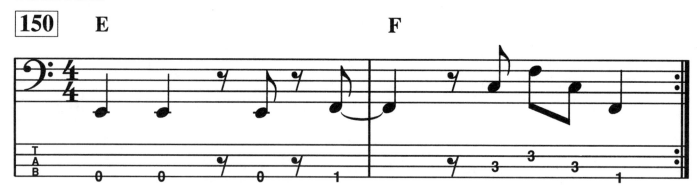

Bossa Nova.

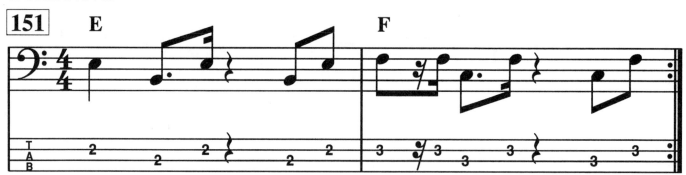

Samba.

Brazilian.

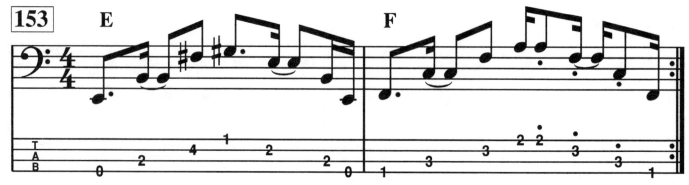

Funky Reggae.

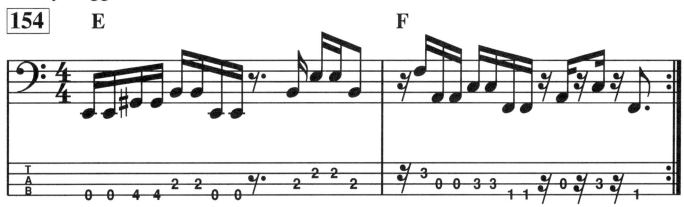

Afro.

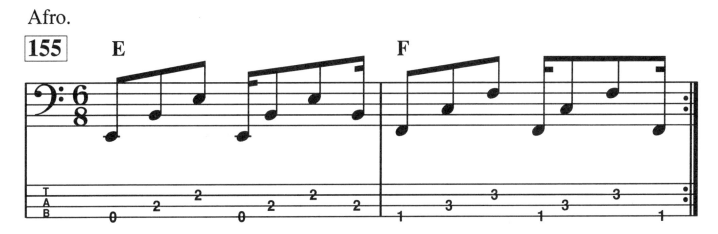

Billy Sheehan

The next eight examples are based upon the same chord progression.
Jazz.

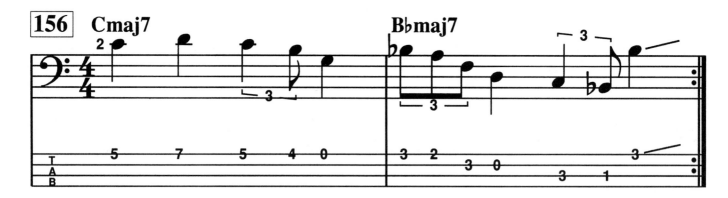

Harmonics chord.

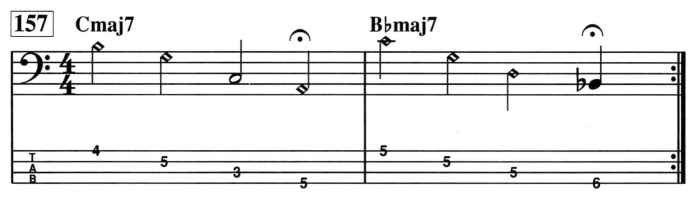

Let all four notes ring.

Samba Rock.

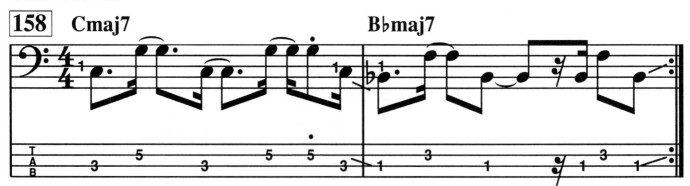

Salsa.

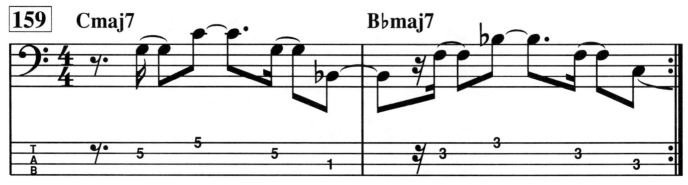

Brazilian.

160 Cmaj7   B♭maj7

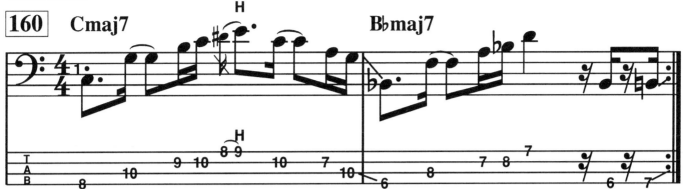

Latin Funk.

161 Cmaj7   B♭maj7

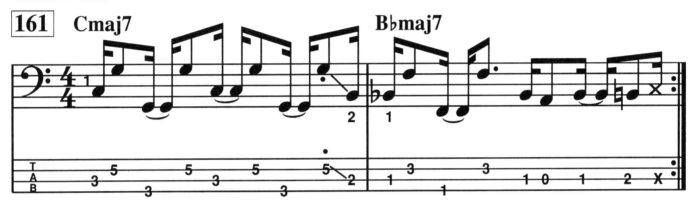

Funk.

162 Cmaj7   B♭maj7

Funk.

163 Cmaj7   B♭maj7

Detuning to the Low D

Tune your E string one tone down to a D note!
The next four examples use this tuning of the low D.

164 Dm

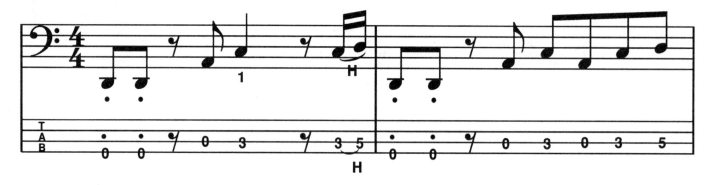

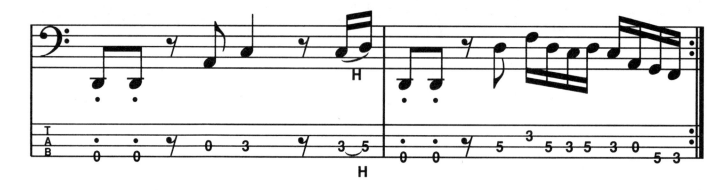

Funky Rock.

165

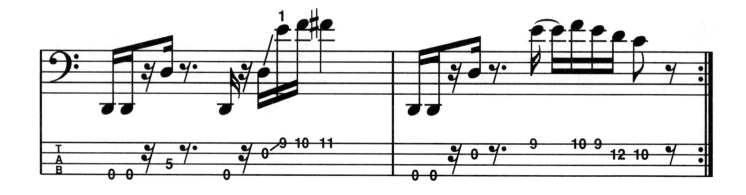

166

Slap

Lick 167 is a variation of Lick 166 using the slap technique.

167

Medium Latin Funk.

168

Blues Lick in F.

169

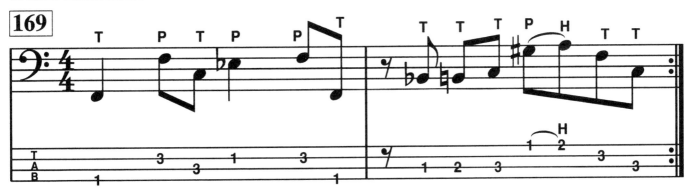

Shuffle.

170 Am   C   G/B

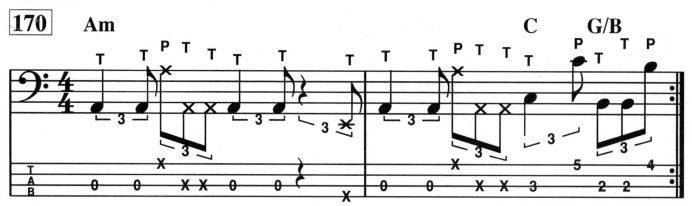

Funk.

171 Am

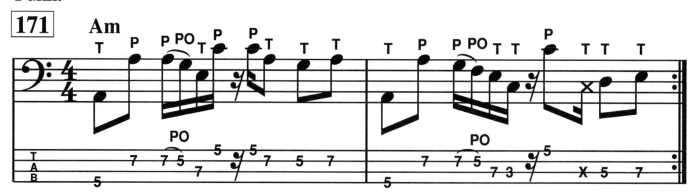

Funky Metal.

172 Am   F   E

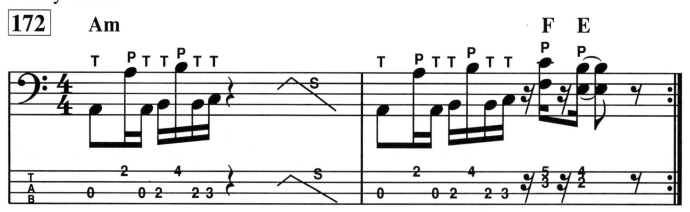

Funky Metal.

173

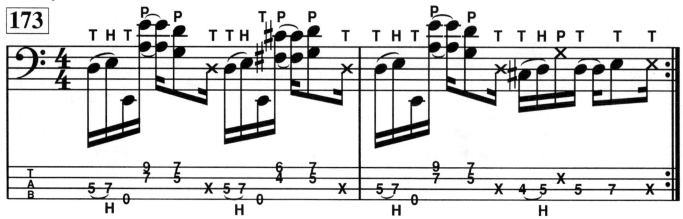

Latin Funk.

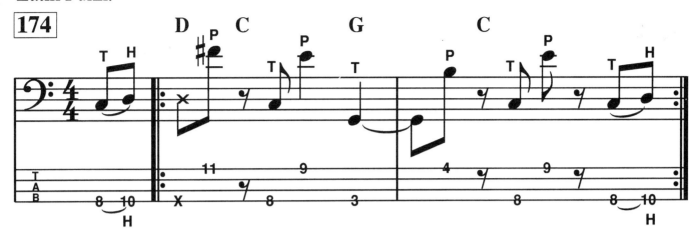

Go Go – accent on one and three, similar to Funk-Rock but using sixteenth note triplets.

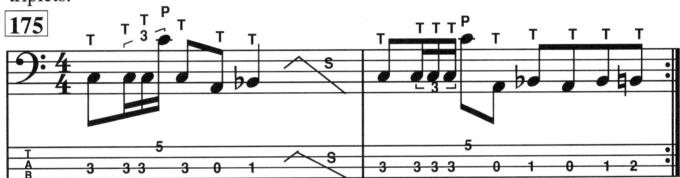

Go go.

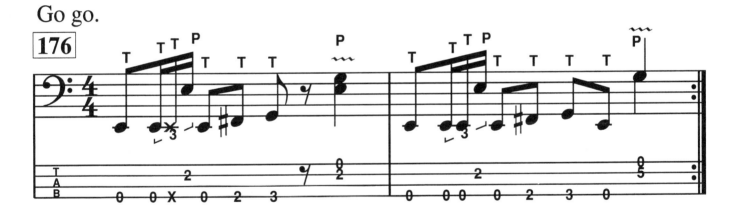

Funk Rock.

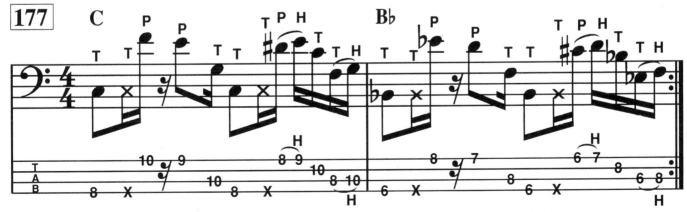

For more information about Slapping see Progressive Slap Technique.

Tapping

Lick 178 is played on the D string only.

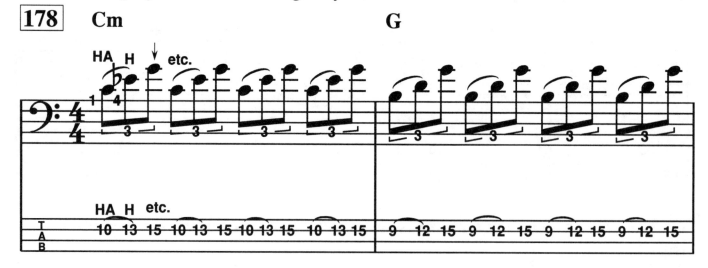

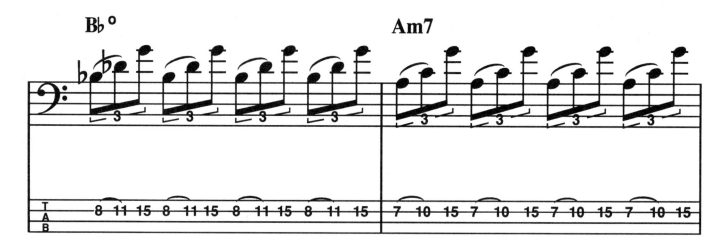

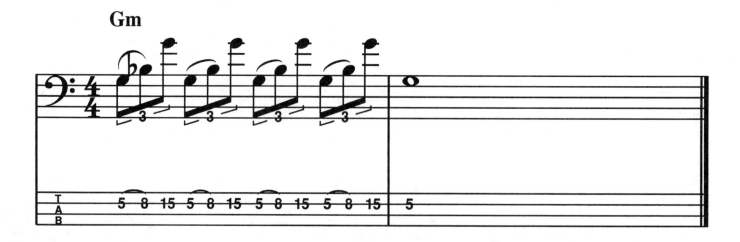

Lick 180 is a variation of Lick 179 using double stops.

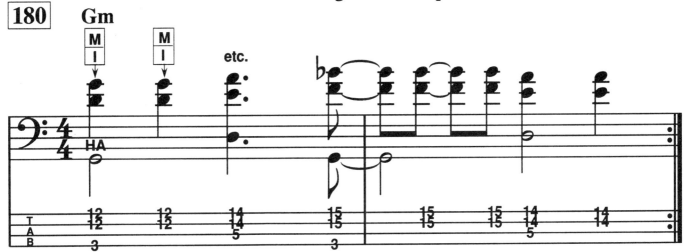

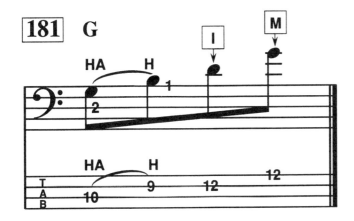

Voicing for Major Chord

For more information about tapping, voicings, chords etc. see Progressive Tapping Technique or Heavy Metal Technique.

Lick 182 uses this major voicing in the first bar.

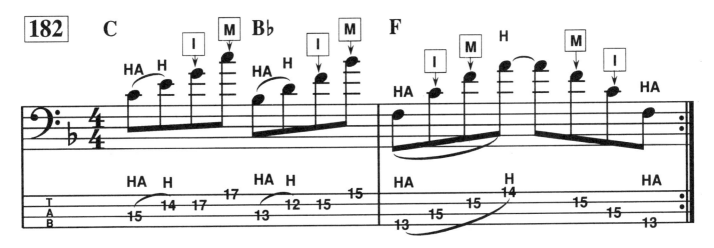

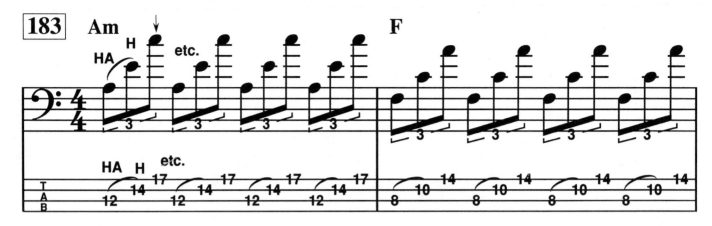

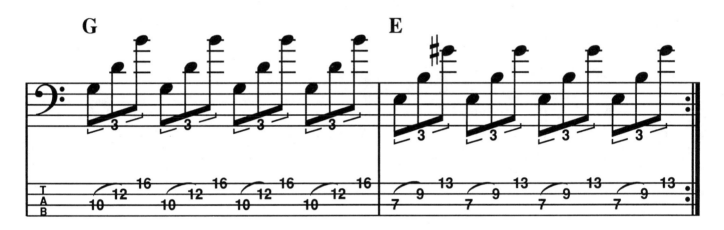

Lick 184 uses cross tapping. For more information see Heavy Metal Technique.

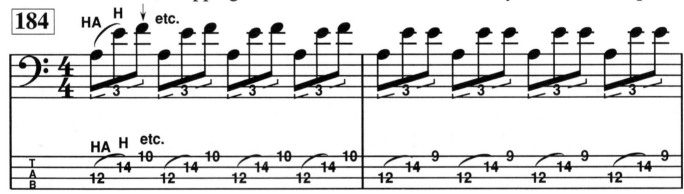

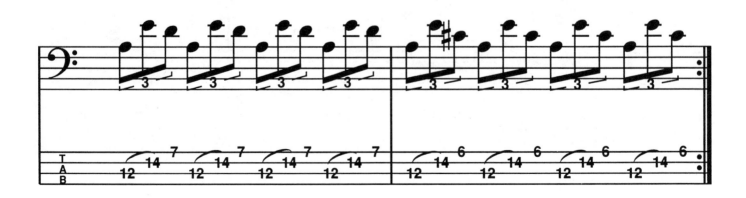

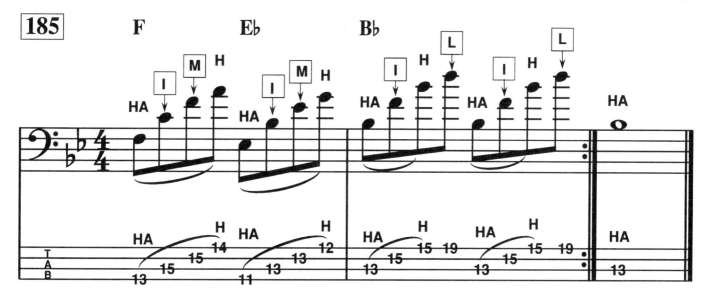

Lick 186 is a variation of the previous lick.

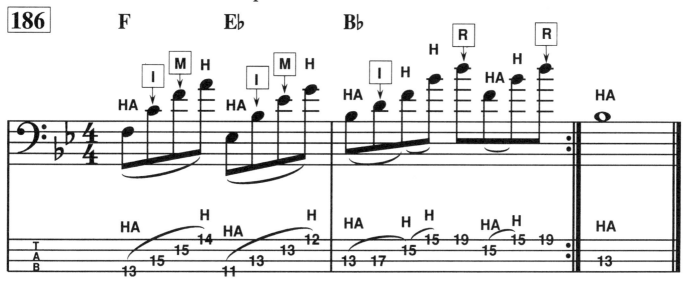

New voicings for the Major, minor and dominant seventh chord.

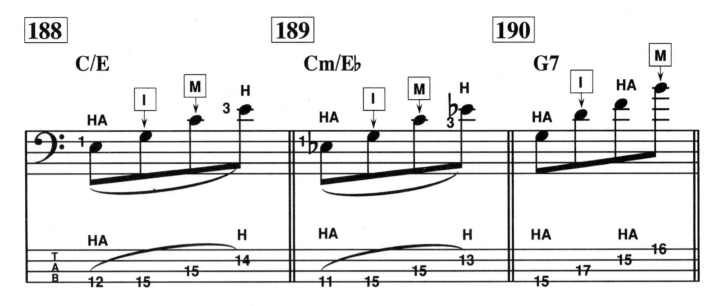

Lick 191 uses new voicings with inversions.

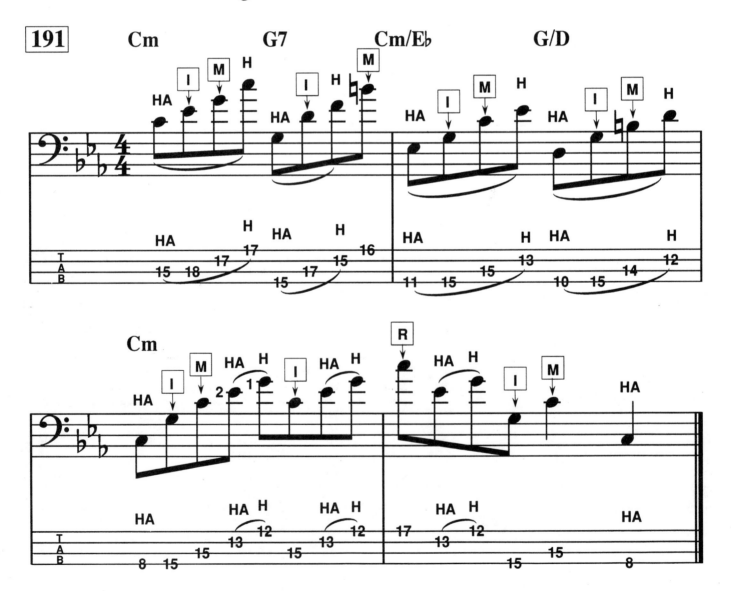